SINK YOUR TEETH INTO

# SHARKS

becker&mayer!

# CONTENTS

# SO MANY SHARKS, SO MANY TEETH

There are more than 400 species, or types, of sharks swimming in the world's oceans. They range in size from the tiny deep-sea dwarf lanternshark, which is just over 6 in. (15 cm) long—about the size of a banana—to the huge whale shark, which is about 40 ft. (12 m) long—or about the size of a school bus.

Not every shark is a big, fast hunting machine that kills and eats anything in its path. Some sharks are bottom-feeders, lying at the bottom of the sea waiting to snatch up prey. Other sharks are tiny and just take nibbles out of larger prey, such as whales. In fact, sharks' diets can be as varied as the types of sharks themselves.

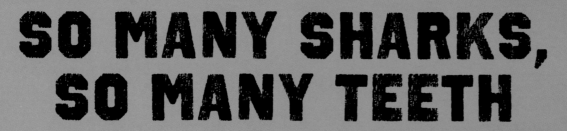

# MY, WHAT USEFUL TEETH YOU HAVE!

The shape of a shark's teeth is related to what it eats. Some sharks, like the great white, have big, jagged, triangular teeth. These teeth are useful for grabbing and tearing through big prey. Other sharks have thin, pointy teeth, perfect for snagging slippery prey like squid. Still other sharks have flat and ridged teeth, good for grinding clams, crabs, and other crustaceans.

## TONS OF TEETH

Most sharks' jaws are filled with rows and rows of teeth. When one tooth falls out, the tooth in the next row moves into its place. Some sharks can lose about 35,000 teeth in a lifetime!

# MORE THAN JUST JAWS

Though its teeth are a shark's most noticeable tools for hunting and feeding, they have plenty of other senses and skills that help them to be the great predators they are.

## SUPER SENSES

- SMELL: Sharks have an excellent sense of smell. It is so good that sharks are sometimes called "swimming noses"! Their nostrils are usually located on the underside of their snout and are used only for smelling, not breathing. Some sharks can smell a single drop of blood in a million drops of water—that's like one tiny drop of perfume in a bathtub!

- HEARING: Sharks have inner ears, which means they don't stick out like a human's do. Sound travels more than four times faster in water than it does in the air, so sharks often rely on hearing to figure out if prey is nearby.

- TOUCH: Sharks have pores that run the length of their bodies. These pores are known as the lateral line. They are filled with cells with small hairs that can sense water pressure and nearby vibrations.

- SIGHT: Sharks can see well in low light. Like cats, they have reflectors in their eyes known as *tapetum lucidum*, which act like mirrors to amplify light.

## OTHER HUNTING TOOLS

- CAMOUFLAGE: Many sharks have white bellies and dark-colored backs. This coloring helps them blend in to the environment. To prey looking down, the shark's dark back blends in with the dark water below. To prey looking up, the shark's white belly helps it blend in with the light water above.

- WHISKERS/BARBELS: Some sharks have whiskers, called barbels, filled with special sensors. The sharks swim close to the ocean bottom, dragging their barbels through the sand to help them detect prey.

- STAYING STILL: To breathe, many sharks must constantly move to allow water to filter through their gills. But some sharks, like nurse sharks, are able to pump water over their gills—so they can stay still at the bottom of the ocean and surprise a tasty meal!

## ELECTROSENSE!

Sharks have special sensory organs known as the *ampullae of Lorenzini*. Through special jelly-filled pores in their heads and along their bodies, sharks can sense weak electrical pulses from nearby creatures. This allows them to detect hidden prey, even creatures buried in the sand.

# GREAT WHITE

## FAST FACTS

6 ft. (1.82 m)

SIZE: 13–22.5 ft. (3.9–6.8 m)

LOCATION: Temperate nearshore waters worldwide

WEIGHT: 1,500–5,000 lbs. (680–2,268 kg)

# JAWS!

Great white sharks are the biggest predatory fish in the sea. These sharks are made for hunting: Their torpedo shape and strong tail let them move through the water at speeds of 25 mph (40 kph), and they have sharp senses that help them locate prey. These excellent hunters also pack a powerful bite. One team of scientists found that a 20-foot (6-m) great white shark could bite with 4,000 lbs. (1,814 kg) of force.

**TOOTH ON THE COVER!**

# Shark Bite File #1

A great white's jaw contains up to 300 large, sharp, triangular teeth. They have jagged edges perfect for biting into large prey such as seals, sea lions, sea turtles, fish, and other marine mammals.

# BULL SHARK

## FAST FACTS

6 ft. (1.82 m)

SIZE: 7-11 ft. (2-3.4 m)

LOCATION:

Shallow, warm
water worldwide

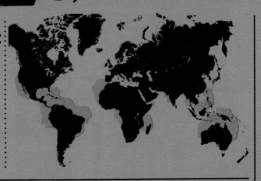

WEIGHT: 200-500 lbs. (90-230 kg)

# WORLD'S DEADLIEST

Did you think the most dangerous shark in the world is the great white? That scary title actually goes to the bull shark. So named because of their short, rounded noses and hot personalities, bull sharks are aggressive and patrol shallow waters along populated coastlines. They are responsible for the majority of shark attacks on humans.

## Shark Bite File #2

Bull sharks' triangular, jagged teeth are great for ripping into bony fish and other sharks, but are also capable of snapping into big prey such as dolphins. These aggressive sharks will eat just about anything: crustaceans, rays, sea birds—even license plates and other junk have been found in their stomachs.

# PORBEAGLE

## FAST FACTS

6 ft. (1.82 m)

**SIZE:** 12 ft. (3.6 m)

**LOCATION:**

Temperate nearshore waters worldwide

**WEIGHT:** 500 lbs. (226 kg)

# ONE COOL SHARK

At first glance, you might think this shark is a mini great white. But it's really its cousin, the porbeagle. One way to tell the difference between the two, aside from size, is that porbeagles have a unique shape to their dorsal, or top, fins. It forms a little tip before connecting to the shark, making it look a little separated. It also has a white or lighter gray area there. Porbeagles can show up where lots of sharks can't: frigid waters. They're able to do this by keeping a body temp that's warmer than the water around them.

## PLAYFUL PREDATORS?

Porbeagles been observed in large groups, seeming to nudge and throw around ocean debris, for no clear reason. That leaves some scientists wondering: Do these sharks like to play?

## Shark Bite File #3

Porbeagle's teeth slice through prey like a knife. They're triangular and pointed, with little extra teeth on either side. These strong chompers are perfect for snaring the large bony fish that porbeagles like to eat.

# SAND TIGER SHARK

## FAST FACTS

6 ft. (1.82 m)

SIZE: 4-10 ft. (1.2-3 m)

LOCATION: Warm waters worldwide, except for the eastern Pacific Ocean

WEIGHT: 200-350 lbs. (91-159 kg)

# TAME TIGERS

Sand tiger sharks look like ferocious man-eaters: Rows of spiny teeth stick out from their open mouths, and their beady eyes eerily scan everything they see. But believe it or not, these scary-looking sharks are not aggressive and attack humans only if they're provoked. They hang out in the shallows and on the sandy sea floor and hunt prey. That's why they're named *sand* tigers.

## AQUARIUM ATTRACTION

Sand tigers are some of the most popular sharks in aquariums because they do well in captivity. In the wild, their life span is usually 15 years, but in aquariums they can live longer. A shark in a New York aquarium lived to be 43.

**TOOTH ON THE COVER!**

## Shark Bite File #4

Sand tiger sharks have a mouthful of thin, sharp, spiny teeth. These teeth are great for snatching small bony fish, crustaceans, and squid—to swallow whole!

13

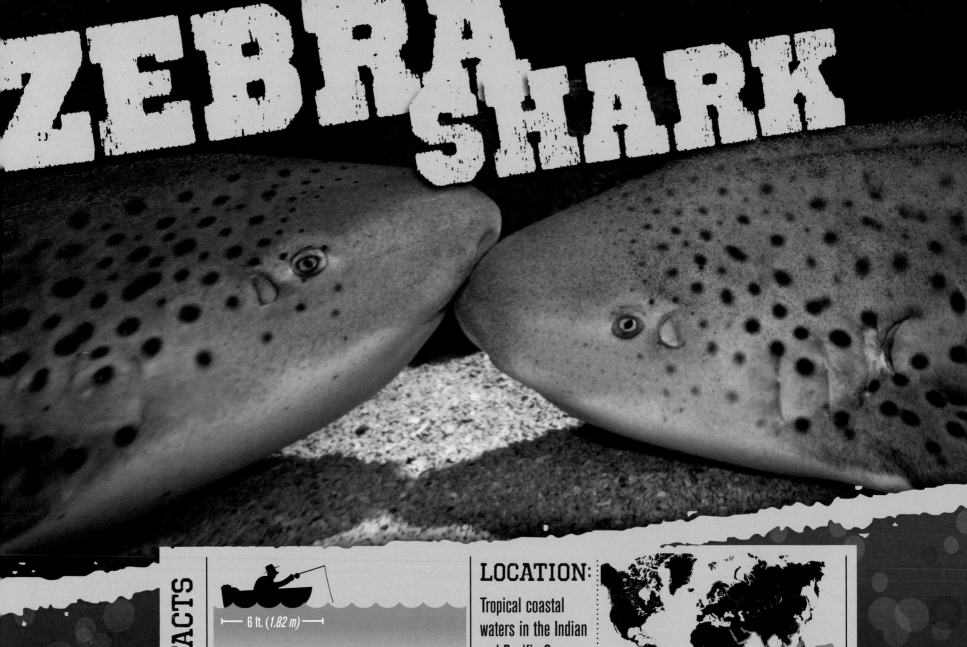

# ZEBRA SHARK

## FAST FACTS

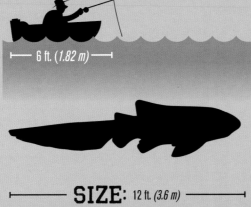

6 ft. (1.82 m)

SIZE: 12 ft. (3.6 m)

LOCATION:
Tropical coastal waters in the Indian and Pacific Oceans

WEIGHT: 44-66 lbs. (20-30 kg)

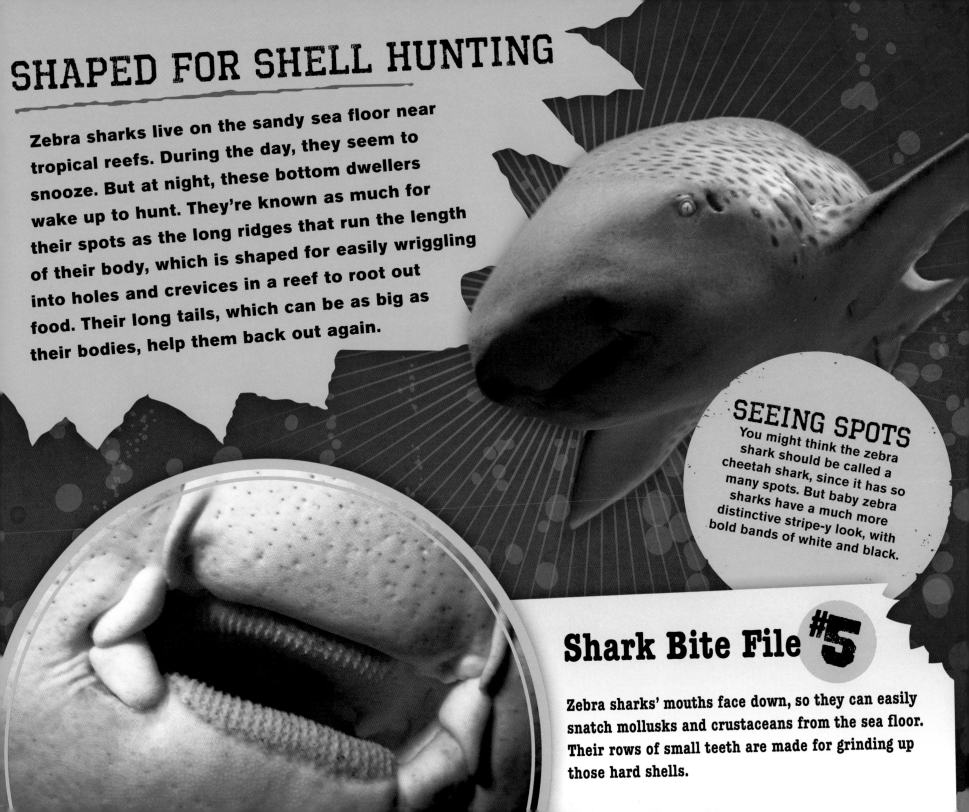

# SHAPED FOR SHELL HUNTING

Zebra sharks live on the sandy sea floor near tropical reefs. During the day, they seem to snooze. But at night, these bottom dwellers wake up to hunt. They're known as much for their spots as the long ridges that run the length of their body, which is shaped for easily wriggling into holes and crevices in a reef to root out food. Their long tails, which can be as big as their bodies, help them back out again.

## SEEING SPOTS

You might think the zebra shark should be called a cheetah shark, since it has so many spots. But baby zebra sharks have a much more distinctive stripe-y look, with bold bands of white and black.

## Shark Bite File #5

Zebra sharks' mouths face down, so they can easily snatch mollusks and crustaceans from the sea floor. Their rows of small teeth are made for grinding up those hard shells.

# COOKIE CUTTER SHARK

## FAST FACTS

6 ft. (1.82 m)

**SIZE:**
1.5–2 ft. (0.5–0.6 m)

**LOCATION:**
Warm ocean waters worldwide, usually near islands

**WEIGHT:** About 7 lbs. (3 kg)

# GLOW-IN-THE-DARK SHARK!

Cookiecutter sharks get their name from the round, cookie-shaped bites they leave in their large prey, such as whales and seals. The ventral side, or belly, of cookiecutter sharks are lined with photophores, which are organs that produce a greenish light. Scientists think these glow-in-the-dark organs help the cookiecutters blend in with the light from the surface of the water and go unnoticed by their prey and other predators.

## HUNGRY FOR A SUB?

Cookiecutter sharks sometimes munch on underwater equipment, such as cables, fishing nets, and even submarines!

## Shark Bite File #6

Cookiecutters' jaws, filled with interconnected triangular teeth, can unhinge to form a circle. The sharks attach themselves to their prey with their suction-like lips, sink in their teeth, and spin around in a circle—leaving that perfect cookie-shaped bite.

17

# TIGER SHARK

**FAST FACTS**

6 ft. *(1.82 m)*

**SIZE:** 10–14 ft. *(3–4.25 m)*

**LOCATION:**

Tropical and subtropical waters throughout the world

**WEIGHT:** 850–1,400 lbs. *(380–640 kg)*

# UNDERWATER TIGERS

Tiger sharks get their name from the dark stripes that appear along their backs. These stripes fade as the sharks age. With a keen sense of smell and great vision, tiger sharks are excellent hunters and eat just about everything they can find, including underwater garbage!

## GARBAGE CAN OF THE SEA

Tiger sharks will eat almost anything. Boots, tires, and trash have been found in their stomachs, earning them the nickname "garbage can of the sea."

## TOOTH ON THE COVER!
## Shark Bite File #7

Tiger sharks have sawlike teeth that are shaped like can openers. In one quick bite, they can easily crack the hard bones and shells of underwater prey like sea turtles.

# GREENLAND SHARK

## FAST FACTS

6 ft. (1.82 m)

SIZE: 8-21 ft. (2.5-6.5 m)

LOCATION: Very limited sightings around the world

WEIGHT: Up to 2,670 lbs. (1,210 kg)

# SLOW MOTIONS

The Greenland shark is the only arctic species of shark and lives in very cold waters. Also known as the sleeper shark, it is a slow mover. In fact, it's the slowest shark in the sea. Some scientists think that these sharks swim so slowly that they can sneak up on snoozing seals, who like to sleep in the water to avoid polar bears. Now, that's one sluggish shark!

## Shark Bite File #8

Greenland sharks have pointy, thin, smooth teeth in their upper jaws and broad, square teeth in their lower jaws. Scientists think these sharks sink their sharp upper teeth into their prey (fish, other sharks, and eels), and then chew in a rolling motion with their bottom teeth.

# HORN SHARK

## FAST FACTS

6 ft. *(1.82 m)*

**SIZE:**
3-4 ft. *(0.9-1.2 m)*

**LOCATION:** Shallow, cool waters in kelp forests off the western U.S.

**WEIGHT:** About 20 lbs. *(9.1 kg)*

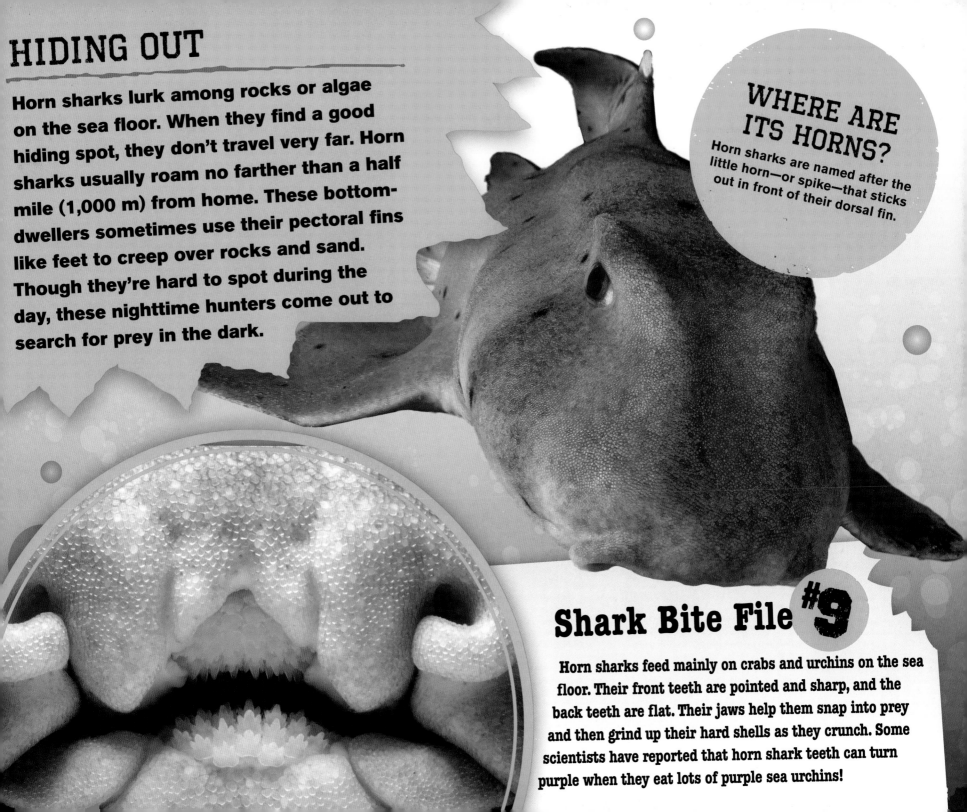

# HIDING OUT

Horn sharks lurk among rocks or algae on the sea floor. When they find a good hiding spot, they don't travel very far. Horn sharks usually roam no farther than a half mile (1,000 m) from home. These bottom-dwellers sometimes use their pectoral fins like feet to creep over rocks and sand. Though they're hard to spot during the day, these nighttime hunters come out to search for prey in the dark.

## WHERE ARE ITS HORNS?

Horn sharks are named after the little horn—or spike—that sticks out in front of their dorsal fin.

## Shark Bite File #9

Horn sharks feed mainly on crabs and urchins on the sea floor. Their front teeth are pointed and sharp, and the back teeth are flat. Their jaws help them snap into prey and then grind up their hard shells as they crunch. Some scientists have reported that horn shark teeth can turn purple when they eat lots of purple sea urchins!

# BLACKTIP REEF SHARK

## FAST FACTS

6 ft. (1.82 m)

**SIZE:** 5-6 ft. (1.5-1.8 m)

**LOCATION:** Near coral reefs in the tropical waters of the Pacific and Indian Oceans

**WEIGHT:** Up to 30 lbs. (13.5 kg)

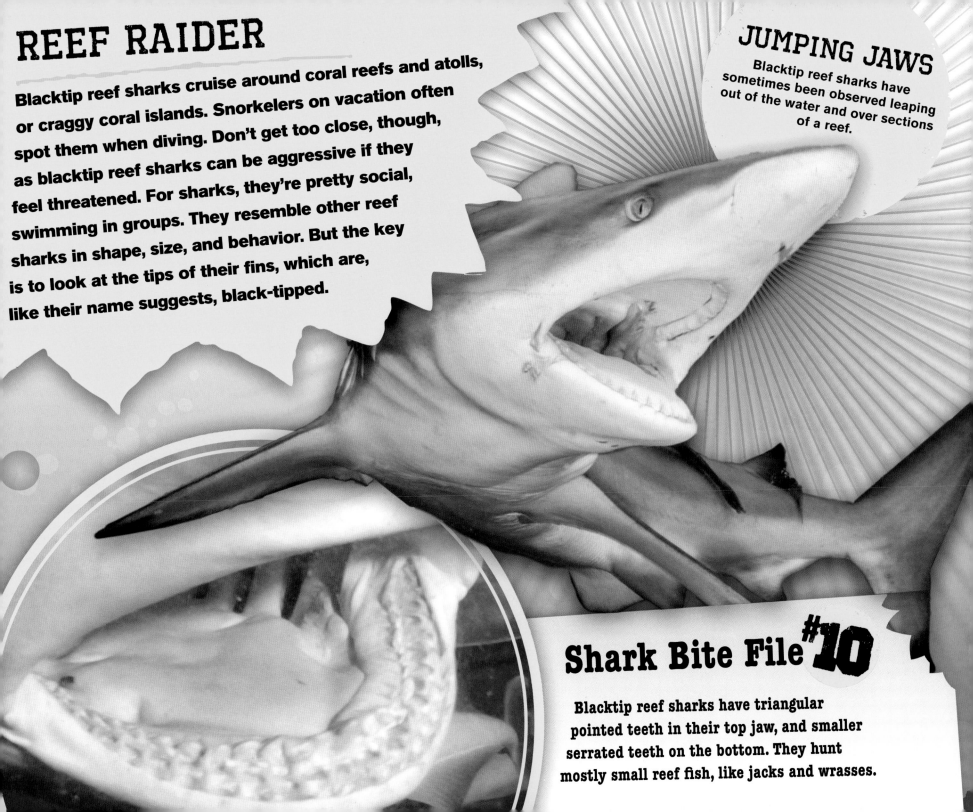

# REEF RAIDER

Blacktip reef sharks cruise around coral reefs and atolls, or craggy coral islands. Snorkelers on vacation often spot them when diving. Don't get too close, though, as blacktip reef sharks can be aggressive if they feel threatened. For sharks, they're pretty social, swimming in groups. They resemble other reef sharks in shape, size, and behavior. But the key is to look at the tips of their fins, which are, like their name suggests, black-tipped.

## JUMPING JAWS

Blacktip reef sharks have sometimes been observed leaping out of the water and over sections of a reef.

## Shark Bite File #10

Blacktip reef sharks have triangular pointed teeth in their top jaw, and smaller serrated teeth on the bottom. They hunt mostly small reef fish, like jacks and wrasses.

# SAWSHARK

## FAST FACTS

6 ft. (1.82 m)

**SIZE:**
About 5.6 ft. (1.7 m)

**LOCATION:**
Mostly in waters near South Africa, Australia, and Japan

**WEIGHT:** UNKNOWN

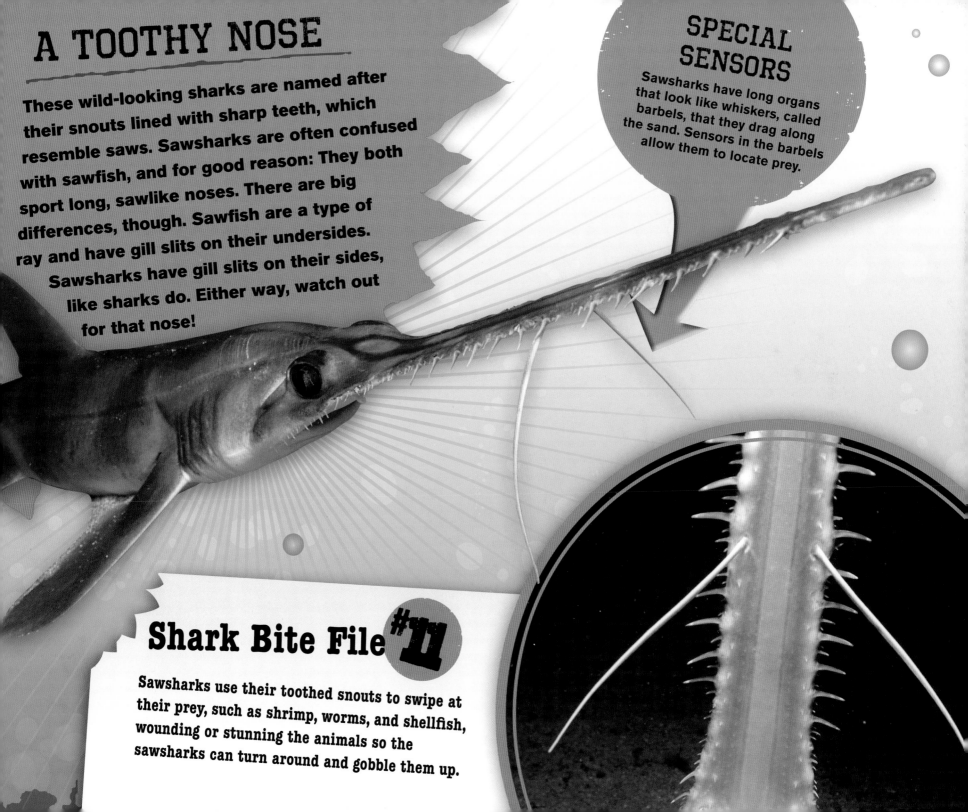

# A TOOTHY NOSE

These wild-looking sharks are named after their snouts lined with sharp teeth, which resemble saws. Sawsharks are often confused with sawfish, and for good reason: They both sport long, sawlike noses. There are big differences, though. Sawfish are a type of ray and have gill slits on their undersides. Sawsharks have gill slits on their sides, like sharks do. Either way, watch out for that nose!

## SPECIAL SENSORS

Sawsharks have long organs that look like whiskers, called barbels, that they drag along the sand. Sensors in the barbels allow them to locate prey.

## Shark Bite File #11

Sawsharks use their toothed snouts to swipe at their prey, such as shrimp, worms, and shellfish, wounding or stunning the animals so the sawsharks can turn around and gobble them up.

# BASKING SHARK

## FAST FACTS

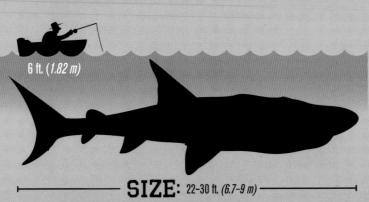

6 ft. (1.82 m)

SIZE: 22-30 ft. (6.7-9 m)

LOCATION: Coastal arctic and temperate waters worldwide

WEIGHT: About 11,000 lbs. (5,180 kg)

# GENTLE GIANTS

Basking sharks can be huge, reaching lengths of close to 40 ft. (12 m)—that's almost as big as a school bus! These massive sharks have hundreds of tiny teeth, but they don't use them for biting. Basking sharks are primarily filter-feeders. They have huge gill slits that go almost completely around their heads, filtering up to 2,000 tons (1,812 mTs) of water in an hour.

## THE MORE THE MERRIER

Unlike most sharks, which prefer to be alone, basking sharks often form groups, or schools. These schools can be made up of a few sharks or up to 100!

## Shark Bite File #12

Basking sharks open their massive mouths—which can reach up to nearly 4 ft. (1.2 m)—and swim to eat, straining small fish, eggs, and plankton through little screens called gill rakers.

# FRILLED SHARK

## FAST FACTS

6 ft. (1.82 m)

### SIZE:
5-6 ft. (2 m)

### LOCATION:
Cold, deep waters at the bottom of the ocean

### WEIGHT: UNKNOWN

# LIVING FOSSIL

Named for its frilly-looking gill slits that allow it to breathe in great ocean depths, the frilled shark is rarely seen alive. Long and eel-like, they usually surface only after they have died. These deep-dwelling sharks are called "living fossils" because they have many primitive features that haven't changed in millions of years.

## Shark Bite File #13

Frilled sharks have large mouths full of 25 rows of multi-pronged, needle-sharp teeth. These teeth make it hard for octopus, squid, and other cephalopods to break loose once the frilled shark sinks its teeth in.

# BLUE SHARK

## FAST FACTS

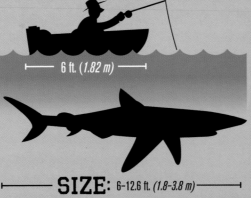

6 ft. (1.82 m)

SIZE: 6-12.6 ft. (1.8-3.8 m)

LOCATION: Temperate ocean waters worldwide

WEIGHT: 60-120 lbs. (27-55 kg)

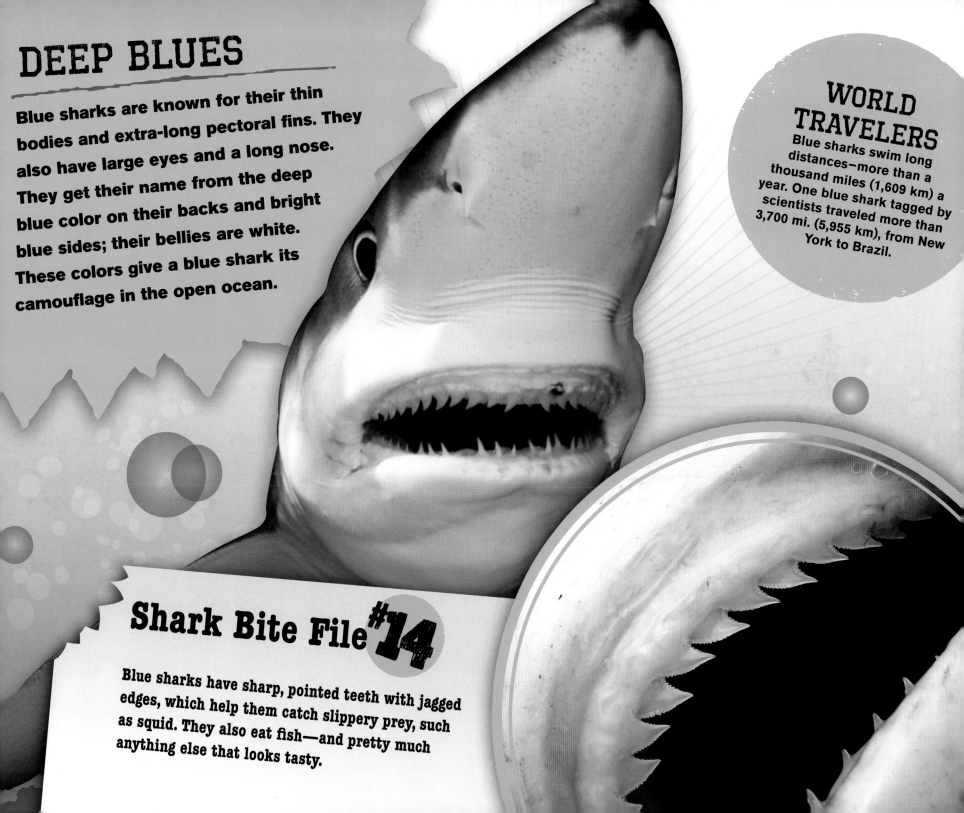

# DEEP BLUES

Blue sharks are known for their thin bodies and extra-long pectoral fins. They also have large eyes and a long nose. They get their name from the deep blue color on their backs and bright blue sides; their bellies are white. These colors give a blue shark its camouflage in the open ocean.

## WORLD TRAVELERS

Blue sharks swim long distances—more than a thousand miles (1,609 km) a year. One blue shark tagged by scientists traveled more than 3,700 mi. (5,955 km), from New York to Brazil.

## Shark Bite File #14

Blue sharks have sharp, pointed teeth with jagged edges, which help them catch slippery prey, such as squid. They also eat fish—and pretty much anything else that looks tasty.

# WOBBEGONG SHARK

## FAST FACTS

6 ft. (1.82 m)

**SIZE:** 5-10 ft. (1.5-3 m)

**LOCATION:** Shallow waters around Australia and Asia

**WEIGHT:** Up to 150 lbs. (70 kg)

# HIDDEN HUNTERS

Wobbegong sharks are a type of carpet shark, with flat bodies and a mottled pattern on their skin. These large sharks use their strange looks to their advantage. Their skin markings and frills help them blend into the sea floor and reefs, where they lie very still until prey swims by. Then they bite!

## Shark Bite File #15

Wobbegong sharks have super-sharp teeth, often described as fangs. These night feeders hunt bottom-dwelling animals such as crabs and lobsters, as well as octopus and larger fish like sea bass.

# THRESHER SHARK

## FAST FACTS

6 ft. (1.82 m)

**SIZE:** 20-25 ft. (6.1-7.6 m), including tail

**LOCATION:** Cool waters along coasts and in open oceans worldwide

**WEIGHT:** Up to 750 lbs. (340 kg)

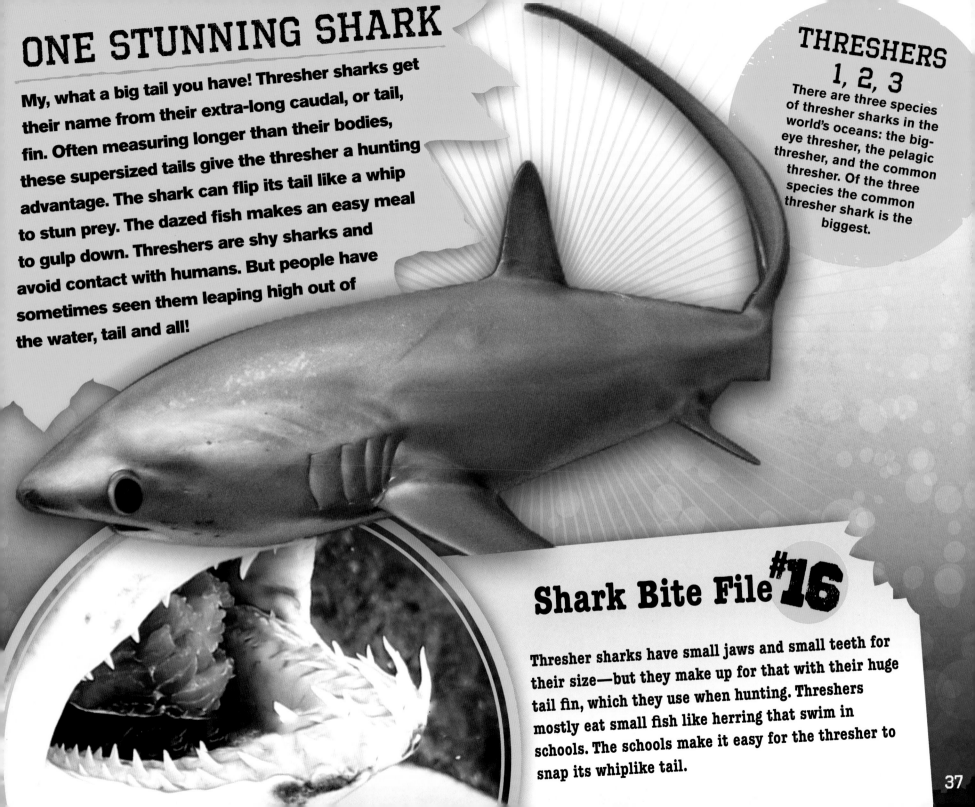

# ONE STUNNING SHARK

My, what a big tail you have! Thresher sharks get their name from their extra-long caudal, or tail, fin. Often measuring longer than their bodies, these supersized tails give the thresher a hunting advantage. The shark can flip its tail like a whip to stun prey. The dazed fish makes an easy meal to gulp down. Threshers are shy sharks and avoid contact with humans. But people have sometimes seen them leaping high out of the water, tail and all!

## THRESHERS 1, 2, 3

There are three species of thresher sharks in the world's oceans: the big-eye thresher, the pelagic thresher, and the common thresher. Of the three species the common thresher shark is the biggest.

## Shark Bite File #16

Thresher sharks have small jaws and small teeth for their size—but they make up for that with their huge tail fin, which they use when hunting. Threshers mostly eat small fish like herring that swim in schools. The schools make it easy for the thresher to snap its whiplike tail.

37

# GREAT HAMMERHEAD SHARK

## FAST FACTS

6 ft. (1.82 m)

**SIZE:** 11.5–20 ft. (3.5–6 m)

**LOCATION:**

Tropical waters worldwide

**WEIGHT:** 500–990 lbs. (227–450 kg)

# HANDY HAMMERHEADS

Great hammerheads are the largest type of hammerhead sharks, identified by their straight, wide heads. Their hammer-shaped noggins are called cephalofoils. Scientists think cephalofoils have many different uses. They may help the sharks swim better, sense prey more easily with spread-out electrical sensors in their nose, or help them to pin down their favorite prey, stingrays. Yum!

## STINGING SUPPER
One of the great hammerhead's favorite foods is the stingray, which it eats whole—tail and all. Stingray tail barbs are often found stuck in great hammerheads' mouths.

## Shark Bite File #17

Great hammerheads aren't picky eaters and will gobble up many marine animals, from lobsters to fish and stingrays to octopus and even other sharks—including other hammerheads!

# GOBLIN SHARK

## FAST FACTS

6 ft. (1.82 m)

**SIZE:** Up to 12.5 Ft. (3.8 M)

**LOCATION:** Off seamounts and continental shelves worldwide

**WEIGHT:** Up to 460 lbs. (208 kg)

# GHOSTLY GOBBLER

You can't miss a goblin shark. With its long, flat nose, tiny eyes, and soft, pinkish body, goblin sharks are definitely one of a kind. They are also very rare deep-sea dwellers. Only 50 have been seen since they were first discovered in the late 1800s.

## Shark Bite File #18

When swimming, goblin sharks have a triangular profile. But when they attack, their jaws are shot forward by special ligaments, allowing their pointed teeth to snare fish, shrimp, and squid.

# MEGAMOUTH SHARK

## FAST FACTS

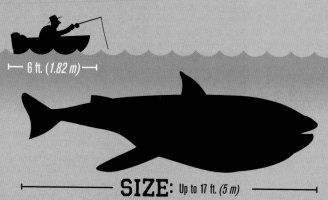

6 ft. *(1.82 m)*

**SIZE:** Up to 17 ft. *(5 m)*

**LOCATION:** Very limited sightings around the world

**WEIGHT:** Up to 2,670 lbs. *(1,210 kg)*

# MYSTERIOUS MEGAMOUTH

Very little is known about this rare shark. In fact, only 55 of them have ever been seen or caught since they were first discovered in 1976. Here's some of what scientists do know: Megamouth sharks live deep down in the water and may sometimes travel upward at night to feed. They have huge mouths (hence the name) and rubbery lips. They're not the best swimmers—they're kind of slow and awkward.

## Shark Bite File #19

The megamouth is a filter-feeder. It opens and extends its huge jaws to let in water filled with small and microscopic creatures, like krill and plankton. The water then filters out through its gills while the shark's screenlike gill rakers hold in the food.

# WHALE SHARK

## FAST FACTS

6 ft. (1.82 m)

**SIZE:** 20-30 ft. (6-9 m) and bigger!

**LOCATION:** All warm tropical waters except the Mediterranean

**WEIGHT:** Average 21 tons (19 tonnes)

# SUPERSIZE SHARK

Whale sharks are not related to whales, but they are just about as big. The largest species of shark, and the largest fish in the sea, these giants average about 20–30 ft. (6–9 m) long. The largest ever measured was over 40 ft. (12 m), and scientists think they grow even bigger, maybe even up to 65 ft. (20 m). That's the length of two buses parked end to end!

## Shark Bite File #20

Whale sharks' jaws can be up to 5 ft. (1.5 m) wide and hold about 300 rows of teeth. But those teeth are tiny and do not appear to play a part in the shark's diet. These supersize filter-feeders eat microscopic plankton or small schooling fish.

# AN OCEAN OF PREDATORS

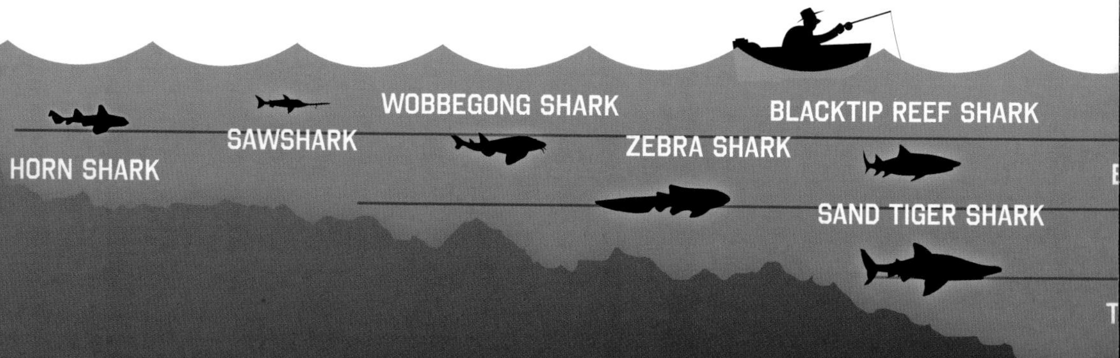

HORN SHARK

SAWSHARK

WOBBEGONG SHARK

ZEBRA SHARK

BLACKTIP REEF SHARK

SAND TIGER SHARK

THERE ARE ABOUT 400 SPECIES OF SHARKS THAT SWIM THE OCEANS, AND MORE ARE BEING DISCOVERED ALL THE TIME. THIS DIAGRAM SHOWS THE DEPTHS AT WHICH SOME OF THE SHARKS IN THIS BOOK HAVE BEEN OBSERVED IN THE WORLD'S OCEANS, FROM THE GREAT WHITE, WHICH CRUISES IN THE OPEN SEA, TO THE TIGER SHARK, WHICH CAN SWIM CLOSE TO SHORE.

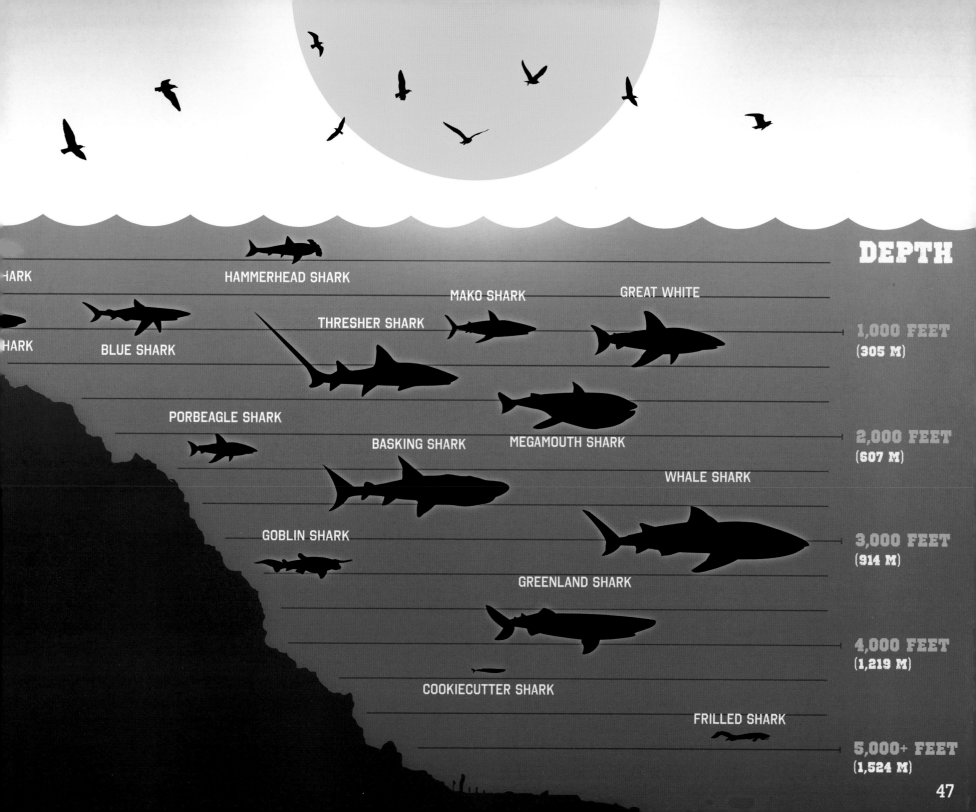

DEPTH

...HARK

HAMMERHEAD SHARK

MAKO SHARK

GREAT WHITE

THRESHER SHARK

...HARK

BLUE SHARK

1,000 FEET
(305 M)

PORBEAGLE SHARK

BASKING SHARK

MEGAMOUTH SHARK

2,000 FEET
(607 M)

WHALE SHARK

GOBLIN SHARK

3,000 FEET
(914 M)

GREENLAND SHARK

4,000 FEET
(1,219 M)

COOKIECUTTER SHARK

FRILLED SHARK

5,000+ FEET
(1,524 M)

*For Miles, who is helping to save the whale sharks.*

Brimming with creative inspiration, how-to projects, and useful information to enrich your everyday life, Quarto Knows is a favorite destination for those pursuing their interests and passions. Visit our site and dig deeper with our books into your area of interest: Quarto Creates, Quarto Cooks, Quarto Homes, Quarto Lives, Quarto Drives, Quarto Explores, Quarto Gifts, or Quarto Kids.

© 2019 Quarto Publishing Group USA Inc.
Produced in 2019 by becker&mayer!, an imprint of The Quarto Group,
11120 NE 33rd Place, Suite 201, Bellevue, WA 98004 USA.
**www.QuartoKnows.com**

19 20 21 22 23  5 4 3 2 1

ISBN: 978-0-7603-6586-1
Library of Congress Cataloging-in-Publication Data available upon request.

Author: L.J. Tracosas
Editor: Leah Jenness
Designer: Sam Dawson and Ava Correa
Photo researcher: Kara Stokes
Product developer: Peter Schumacher
Production coordinator: Tom Miller

Printed, manufactured, and assembled in Shenzhen, China, 06/19
Complies with CPSIA

Distributed by:
Scholastic Inc., New York, NY 10012
Scholastic Canada Ltd., Markham, Ontario L6C 1Z7
Scholastic New Zealand Ltd., East Tamaki, Auckland 2013
Scholastic Australia Pty. Ltd., Gosford, NSW, 2250
Scholastic UK, Southam, Warwickshire CV47 0RA

MIX
Paper from responsible sources
FSC® C017606
www.fsc.org

Image credits:
Cover: Great white shark © SeaPics.com. Title page: Shark teeth © Pinosub/Shutterstock © Bliss Hunter Images/Shutterstock. Page 3: Great white shark © Jim Agronick/Shutterstock. Page 4: Porbeagle teeth © Chris & Monique Fallows Nature Picture Library/Alamy © Kelvin Aitkin/Visual&Written SL/Alamy; blue shark teeth © Mark Conlin/Alamy; goblin shark teeth © SeaPics.com; tiger shark teeth © SeaPics.com; great white shark teeth © SeaPics.com. Page 5: Caribbean reef shark © Rich Carey/Shutterstock. Page 6: Great white shark © James D Watt/Stephen Frink Collection/Alamy. Page 7: Great white shark teeth, same as page 4; great white shark close up © SeaPics.com. Page 8: Bull shark © Michael Patrick O'Neill/Alamy. Page 9: Bull shark teeth © NORBERT WU/MINDEN PICTURES/National Geographic Creative; bull shark open mouth © SeaPics.com. Page 10: Porbeagle shark © Doug Perrine/Getty Images. Page 11: Mako shark teeth, same as page 4; Porbeagle shark open mouth © Maddie Meyer/Getty Images. Page 12: Sand tiger shark © SeaPics.com. Page 13: Sand tiger teeth © SeaPics.com. Page 14: Zebra shark © Mathieu Meur/Stocktrek Images/Getty Images. Page 15: Zebra shark teeth © Jeff Rotman/Getty Images; zebra shark © Stephanie Starr / EyeEm/Getty Images. Page 16: Cookiecutter shark © Courtesy George Burgess. Page 17: Cookiecutter shark © Courtesy Karsten Hartel/Marine Fisheries Review/NOAA via Wikimedia Commons; cookiecutter shark bite © SeaPics.com. Page 18: Tiger shark © JIM ABERNETHY/National Geographic Creative. Page 19: Tiger shark teeth, same as page 4; tiger shark grin © Franco Banfi/Getty Images. Page 20: Greenland shark © SeaPics.com. Page 21: Greenland shark mouth © WaterFram/Alamy. Page 22: Horn Shark © KGrif/Shutterstock. Page 23: horn shark teeth © SeaPics.com; horn shark © Kirk Wester/Shutterstock. Page 24: Blacktip reef shark © Ian Scott/Shutterstock. Page 25: blacktip reef shark © Dray van Beeck/Shutterstock; blacktip reef shark mouth © Barcroft/Getty Images.com. Page 26: Sawshark © Mary Snyderman/Stephen Frink Collection/Alamy. Page 27: Sawshark teeth, same as page 26; sawshark toothy nose © Mary Snyderman/Stephen Frink Collection/Alamy. Page 28: Basking shark © SeaPics.com. Page 29: Basking shark open mouth © SeaPics.com. Page 30: Frilled shark © SeaPics.com. Page 31: Frilled shark body © Getty Images/Staff/Getty Images. Page 32: Blue shark © SeaPics.com. Page 33: Blue shark open mouth © JIM ABERNETHY/National Geographic Creative; blue shark teeth, same as page 4. Page 34: Wobbegong shark © WaterFrame/Alamy. Page 35: Wobbegong shark close up © Jeff Rotman/Oxford Scientific/Getty Images; wobbegong shark open mouth © SeaPics.com. Page 36: Thresher shark © Shane Gross/Shutterstock. Page 37: thresher shark mouth © Maddie Meyer/Getty Images; thresher shark © SeaPics.com. Page 38: Great hammerhead shark © SeaPics.com. Page 39: Great hammerhead shark open mouth © SeaPics.com; great hammerhead shark teeth © SeaPics.com. Page 40: Goblin shark © SeaPics.com. Page 41: Goblin shark mouth © SeaPics.com; goblin shark teeth, same as page 4. Page 42: Megamouth shark © SeaPics.com. Page 43: Megamouth closeup © SeaPics.com; megamouth teeth © SeaPics.com. Page 44: Whale shark feeding © SeaPics.com. Page 45: Whale shark open mouth © MAURICIO HANDLER/National Geographic Creative; whale shark mouth close up © SeaPics.com. Page 48: Shark © Willyam Bradberry/Shutterstock.

Design elements used throughout:
Abstract circles © javi merino/Shutterstock; tropical plant silhouettes © OKSANA/Shutterstock; seagull silhouette © SCOTTCHAN/Shutterstock; underwater tropical reef © EpicStockMedia/Shutterstock.

306140